Title: The Power of Universal Love: Cultivating Compassion and Connection for a Happier Life

This book explores the concept of universal love, its various forms, and how to cultivate it for personal and societal wellbeing. The chapters delve into the differences between universal love and other forms of love, such as romantic and familial love, and how it is practiced in different spiritual traditions. The scientific research on the benefits of practicing universal love, such as improved emotional and physical health, is also examined. Additionally, the book provides practical tips for overcoming common obstacles to practicing universal love, integrating it into daily life, and creating a more compassionate and connected society. A bonus chapter explores the application of universal love in management and how it can lead to a culture of trust and respect in the workplace. Overall, this book aims to inspire readers to make universal love a habit and create a more peaceful and harmonious world.

Introduction:

Explanation of the concept of universal love and its importance for personal and societal wellbeing: Universal love, also known as unconditional love or divine love, is a concept that transcends the traditional notion of love as an emotion or feeling shared between two people. Instead, universal love is an all-encompassing force that connects all living beings and recognizes that each one of us is interconnected and interdependent. The concept of universal love is often associated with compassion, empathy, and loving-kindness, which are practices that help cultivate this all-embracing form of love.

Cultivating universal love has numerous benefits for personal and societal wellbeing. On an individual level, practicing universal love can lead to greater emotional resilience, improved relationships, increased empathy and compassion, and a greater sense of connectedness and meaning in life. For instance, research has shown that practicing loving-kindness meditation can help reduce symptoms of depression, anxiety, and post-traumatic stress disorder (PTSD). Moreover, cultivating universal love can improve the quality of interpersonal relationships, including those with loved ones, coworkers, and even strangers.

On a societal level, universal love is essential for creating a more compassionate and connected world. When individuals cultivate universal love, they become more empathetic and compassionate towards others, which reduces conflict and violence, encourages cooperation and collaboration, and promotes greater harmony and understanding between people. In this way, universal love has the potential to transform not only individuals but also entire communities and even nations.

Overview of the book's structure and content:

The book is structured into seven chapters, each of which explores different aspects of universal love in-depth:

Chapter 1: What is Universal Love? This chapter defines and explains the concept of universal love and its benefits. It also discusses the differences between universal love and other forms of love, such as romantic love and familial love.

Chapter 2: Forms of Universal Love. This chapter delves into different forms of universal love, such as loving-kindness, compassion, and empathy, and how they can be practiced in daily life. It also provides examples of how each form of universal love can improve personal and societal wellbeing.

Chapter 3: Cultivating Universal Love for Self and Others. This chapter discusses how to cultivate universal love for oneself and others, including loved ones, strangers, and even difficult people. It explores the importance of non-judgment and empathy in cultivating universal love and provides practical tips for integrating these practices into daily life.

Chapter 4: Universal Love in Spiritual Traditions. This chapter explores the role of universal love in various spiritual traditions, such as Buddhism, Hinduism, Christianity, and Islam. It discusses how universal love is practiced in these traditions and how it can be adapted to fit different cultural and religious contexts.

Chapter 5: Science of Universal Love. This chapter examines the scientific research on the benefits of practicing universal love. It explores how the practice of loving-kindness meditation can lead to improved emotional and physical health, such as reducing symptoms of depression, anxiety, and PTSD.

Chapter 6: Overcoming Obstacles to Universal Love. This chapter discusses common obstacles to practicing universal love, such as fear, anger, and judgment, and how to overcome them through mindfulness and other techniques. It also emphasizes the importance of self-compassion in overcoming obstacles.

Chapter 7: Living a Life of Universal Love. This final chapter provides practical tips for integrating the practice of universal love into daily life and creating a more compassionate and connected society. It encourages readers to make universal love a habit and outlines the role of universal love in creating a more peaceful and harmonious world.

Bonus Chapter: The Power of Universal Love in Management. This chapter talks about how universal love when applied in business can build strong bonds between management and employees. This culture drive business results but also creates a culture of trust and respect.

Chapter 1: What is Universal Love?

Love is a complex and multifaceted emotion that has been the subject of much exploration and contemplation throughout human history. Traditionally, love has been associated with romantic relationships, familial bonds, and close friendships. However, there is another type of love that goes beyond these traditional relationships - universal love.

Universal love is an all-encompassing force that connects all living beings, recognizing that we are all interconnected and interdependent. It is characterized by compassion, empathy, and loving-kindness towards all, without discrimination based on social status, race, gender, or any other external factor. Universal love recognizes the inherent worth and dignity of all beings and seeks to promote their wellbeing.

The concept of universal love is not limited to any specific culture, religion, or tradition. It can be practiced and cultivated by anyone, regardless of their background. Moreover, cultivating universal love has numerous benefits for personal and societal wellbeing.

Practicing universal love can lead to greater emotional resilience, improved relationships, increased empathy and compassion, and a greater sense of connectedness and meaning in life. Research has shown that practicing loving-kindness meditation can help reduce symptoms of depression, anxiety, and post-traumatic stress disorder (PTSD). Cultivating universal love can also improve the quality of interpersonal relationships, including those with loved ones, coworkers, and even strangers. When we approach others with compassion and empathy, we are more likely to understand their perspectives and needs, which can lead to more harmonious and fulfilling relationships.

While universal love shares some similarities with other forms of love, such as romantic love and familial love, there are also some key differences. Romantic love is often characterized by feelings of attraction, passion, and intimacy, while familial love is often based on shared genetics or upbringing. In contrast, universal love is not based on any external factors. It is an all-encompassing love that recognizes the inherent worth and dignity of all beings, regardless of their social status, race, or gender. Moreover, universal love is not limited to a specific relationship or context. It is a love that can be directed towards all living beings, including strangers and even those who have harmed us in the past.

To cultivate universal love, there are numerous practices that one can engage in. Loving-kindness meditation is one of the most effective practices for cultivating universal love. This practice involves directing loving and kind thoughts towards oneself and others, repeating phrases such as "may I be happy, may I be healthy, may I be at peace" and directing these same phrases towards loved ones, acquaintances, and even difficult people. Compassion meditation is another effective practice for cultivating universal love, which involves directing thoughts and feelings of compassion and empathy towards oneself and others, particularly those who are suffering or in pain.

In addition to meditation practices, there are also numerous daily practices that can help cultivate universal love. Practicing active listening and seeking to understand others' perspectives, performing acts of kindness for strangers, and reframing negative thoughts into positive ones can all help cultivate universal love.

Another way to cultivate universal love is through mindfulness practices. Mindfulness involves paying attention to the present moment with an open and non-judgmental attitude. By practicing mindfulness, we can become more aware of our thoughts and feelings, which can help us cultivate greater empathy and compassion towards ourselves and others.

Moreover, practicing forgiveness can also help cultivate universal love. Forgiveness involves letting go of anger, resentment, and the desire for revenge towards those who have harmed us. By practicing forgiveness, we can cultivate compassion towards those who have caused us pain, which can help us heal and move forward with greater love and understanding.

It is important to note that cultivating universal love is not always easy, particularly when we are faced with difficult situations or individuals who challenge our ability to feel love and compassion. However, by approaching these situations with an open heart and a willingness to learn and grow, we can cultivate greater resilience and strength in our ability to love unconditionally.

Furthermore, it is important to remember that cultivating universal love is not an individual pursuit, but rather a collective one. When we practice universal love, we not only benefit ourselves, but we also contribute to the wellbeing of our communities and the world as a whole. In a world that can often feel divided and disconnected, cultivating universal love can serve as a powerful force for healing and unity.

In conclusion, universal love is an all-encompassing force that recognizes the inherent worth and dignity of all beings. It is a love that transcends external factors such as social status, race, or gender and seeks to promote the wellbeing of all. By practicing loving-kindness meditation, compassion meditation, mindfulness, forgiveness, and other practices, we can cultivate universal love and reap numerous personal and societal benefits. As we continue to cultivate universal love in our own lives, we can contribute to a more compassionate and connected world.

Chapter 2: Forms of Universal Love

Love is a complex emotion that has been the subject of countless studies and investigations throughout history. It is a powerful feeling that can take many forms and have a significant impact on both individuals and society as a whole. However, universal love, a type of love that transcends personal attachments and embraces all living beings, is a distinct and important concept.

Universal love is not restricted to family members, friends, or even romantic partners, but extends to all people and even animals. It is a love that sees the inherent goodness in all living beings and treats them with kindness and compassion. By practicing universal love, we can develop a sense of interconnectedness with all living beings and foster a deep sense of empathy and compassion.

One form of universal love is loving-kindness, also known as metta meditation. This type of meditation involves repeating positive phrases or affirmations to oneself and others, such as "may you be happy" or "may you be at peace." By focusing on positive thoughts and sending good wishes to others, we can cultivate a sense of universal love and compassion. It involves cultivating a deep sense of benevolence towards oneself and others by repeating positive phrases or affirmations. The practice of loving-kindness is a powerful tool that can help us to cultivate a deep sense of inner peace, love, and compassion.

To practice loving-kindness, it is important to find a quiet and comfortable space where you can sit or lie down without any distractions. Begin by focusing your attention on your breath and taking a few deep breaths to help you relax. Once you feel calm and centered, start to repeat positive phrases or affirmations to yourself.

These affirmations can vary depending on what you feel you need in the moment. Some common phrases include:

May I be happy and healthy.

May I be free from suffering.

May I be at peace with myself and others.

May I feel loved and supported.

As you repeat these phrases to yourself, try to really feel the emotions and sentiments behind the words. Visualize yourself surrounded by a warm, glowing light that radiates love and compassion. Allow this feeling of love and kindness to permeate your entire being.

Once you have cultivated a sense of loving-kindness towards yourself, you can then extend it to others. You can start by focusing on someone close to you, such as a family member or friend. Repeat the same phrases to them, replacing "I" with their name. For example:

May [insert name] be happy and healthy.

May [insert name] be free from suffering.

May [insert name] be at peace with themselves and others.

May [insert name] feel loved and supported.

As you extend this practice to others, gradually include more people in your circle of loving-kindness. You can start with those who you find it easy to feel kindness towards, and gradually work towards including more challenging individuals, such as those who have caused you harm or difficulty.

Through the practice of loving-kindness, we can learn to cultivate a deep sense of inner peace, love, and compassion towards ourselves and others. It can help to reduce stress and anxiety, increase feelings of happiness and well-being, and improve relationships with others. This practice is not limited to any particular religion or spiritual tradition and can be practiced by anyone, regardless of their beliefs or background.

Another form of universal love is compassion, which is the ability to feel empathy and concern for others who are suffering. Compassion enables us to put ourselves in other people's shoes and understand their pain and struggles. This allows us to respond with kindness and support, rather than judgment or indifference.

Compassion is a crucial aspect of universal love. It involves feeling empathy and concern for those who are suffering, including both humans and animals. When we practice compassion, we are able to put ourselves in someone else's shoes and understand their pain and struggles. This understanding allows us to respond with kindness and support, rather than judgment or indifference.

Compassion involves both a cognitive and emotional aspect. Cognitively, we recognize that someone is suffering and understand their pain. Emotionally, we feel moved by their suffering and want to alleviate it. This can include offering a listening ear, providing practical help, or simply offering kind words.

When we practice compassion, we not only benefit others, but also ourselves. Studies have shown that compassionate people are more likely to experience positive emotions and have better mental and physical health. They are also more likely to have stronger and more meaningful relationships with others.

Moreover, compassion is not just limited to those we know and love. It extends to all living beings, including strangers and animals. By practicing compassion towards all living beings, we can create a more peaceful and harmonious world.

One way to cultivate compassion is through meditation. This involves focusing on someone who is suffering and imagining sending them love and support. It can also involve actively seeking out opportunities to help others and make a positive impact in the world.

In summary, compassion is an essential component of universal love. By practicing compassion, we can understand and alleviate the suffering of others, create more meaningful relationships, and make the world a more peaceful and harmonious place. Empathy is another form of universal love that involves understanding and sharing the feelings of others. When we practice empathy, we are able to connect with others on a deep level and offer support and comfort when they need it most. This type of love is particularly important in building strong relationships and fostering a sense of community.

Empathy is an important aspect of universal love because it allows us to feel the pain and suffering of others and respond with kindness and support. This is particularly important in situations where someone is going through a difficult time or facing a challenge. When we can empathize with someone, we can offer them comfort and understanding, which can help them feel less alone and more supported.

Practicing empathy can also help us develop deeper and more meaningful relationships with others. When we are able to understand and share the feelings of others, we are better able to communicate and connect with them. This can lead to stronger friendships, romantic relationships, and even professional connections.

One way to practice empathy is to actively listen to others when they are sharing their feelings or experiences with us. This means paying attention to what they are saying, asking clarifying questions, and reflecting back what we have heard to ensure we understand their perspective. It also means being present with them in the moment, without judgment or distractions.

Another way to practice empathy is to put ourselves in other people's shoes and imagine how we would feel in their situation. This can be particularly helpful when someone is going through a difficult time or facing a challenge that we may not have experienced ourselves. By imagining how we would feel in their position, we can better understand their emotions and respond with compassion and support.

Ultimately, practicing empathy is a powerful way to cultivate universal love in our lives. By connecting with others on a deep level and offering support and compassion, we can create a more peaceful and harmonious world.

Practicing the different forms of universal love can have significant positive impacts on both individuals and society. The benefits of loving-kindness meditation and other forms of universal love have been extensively researched, and studies have shown that people who practice these techniques are more likely to experience positive emotions such as happiness, joy, and contentment. Moreover, they tend to have better mental and physical health outcomes, as well as stronger and more meaningful relationships with others.

But the effects of universal love extend beyond just individual wellbeing. By treating all living beings with kindness and compassion, we can create a more harmonious and peaceful world. As we extend our love and compassion to others, we create a ripple effect that spreads beyond our immediate circle of friends and family. This ripple effect can inspire others to act with kindness and compassion towards those around them, creating a domino effect of positive energy that can transform communities and even entire societies.

This is precisely why universal love is such an important concept in many spiritual traditions, such as Buddhism and Hinduism. These traditions recognize that love is a powerful force that can transform individuals and societies alike. By cultivating universal love through practices like loving-kindness meditation, we can become agents of positive change in the world, creating a more

compassionate and connected global community.

Chapter 3: Cultivating Universal Love for Self and Others

Love is often thought of as selflessness and sacrifice, but it is important to remember that love starts with the self. To cultivate universal love, we must first learn to love ourselves. When we have a foundation of self-love, it becomes easier to extend that love to others. This chapter will explore various ways to cultivate universal love for oneself and others.

One way to start cultivating universal love for oneself is by practicing self-compassion. Self-compassion involves treating ourselves with kindness and understanding, much like we would treat a close friend. This means accepting ourselves for who we are, with all our flaws and imperfections, and acknowledging that we are deserving of love and compassion. When we practice self-compassion, we are less likely to engage in negative self-talk and self-criticism, which can hinder our ability to extend love to others. For instance, we can try to talk to ourselves kindly, especially during difficult times. Instead of harshly criticizing ourselves, we can give ourselves gentle and positive affirmations.

Another way to cultivate universal love for oneself is by practicing self-care. Self-care involves taking care of our physical, emotional, and spiritual needs. This can range from something as simple as taking a relaxing bath or going for a walk in nature, to more involved practices like meditation or therapy. By taking care of ourselves, we are demonstrating love and compassion towards ourselves. For example, we can set aside some time for ourselves each day to engage in activities that bring us joy and fulfillment.

Once we have established a foundation of love for ourselves, we can extend that love to others. This involves practicing empathy and compassion towards others, regardless of our personal feelings towards them. One way to cultivate empathy is by actively listening to others and trying to understand their perspective. This means setting aside our own biases and judgments and truly listening to what the other person is saying. We can try to empathize with their situation and imagine what it would be like to be in their shoes.

Compassion involves recognizing the suffering of others and taking action to alleviate it. This can be as simple as offering a listening ear to a friend in need or volunteering at a local charity. By extending compassion towards others, we are demonstrating universal love and creating a more compassionate world. We can practice compassion by engaging in acts of kindness and generosity towards others, even strangers. Small acts of kindness, such as holding the door open for someone or offering to help carry their groceries, can go a long way in demonstrating compassion and love.

Empathy involves actively listening to others and trying to understand their perspective, without judgment or bias. This can be particularly challenging when we disagree with someone or find their actions hurtful. However, by taking the time to listen and understand, we can build stronger relationships and foster a sense of connection with others.

Finally, it is important to note that cultivating universal love is an ongoing process that requires patience and practice. It is not always easy to extend love and compassion towards others, especially in challenging situations. However, by making a conscious effort to practice universal love, we can create a positive ripple effect in our own lives and in the lives of those around us.

In conclusion, cultivating universal love for oneself and others is a powerful tool for creating a more compassionate and connected world. By practicing self-compassion, self-care, empathy, and compassion, we can create a foundation of love that extends far beyond ourselves. It may not always be easy, but the rewards of universal love are immeasurable.

Chapter 4: Universal Love in Spiritual Traditions

The concept of universal love is a powerful principle embraced by many spiritual traditions as a means to achieve greater inner peace, connection, and fulfillment. Let us explore the role of universal love in various spiritual traditions and how it is practiced by their followers.

In Buddhism, universal love is known as metta or loving-kindness. The practice of metta involves extending unconditional love and compassion towards all beings, including oneself, loved ones, strangers, and even enemies. Through the practice of metta, Buddhists seek to overcome the suffering caused by attachment and aversion and cultivate greater inner peace and equanimity. It is one of the four Brahma Viharas or divine abodes, which are states of mind that lead to greater inner peace, equanimity, and happiness. The practice of metta involves reciting phrases of loving-kindness towards oneself and others, visualizing a sense of warmth and openness in the heart, and extending goodwill and compassion towards all beings. Through the practice of metta, Buddhists seek to overcome the suffering caused by attachment and aversion and to cultivate a greater sense of inner peace and equanimity.

In Hinduism, universal love is known as bhakti or devotion. The practice of bhakti involves developing a deep love and devotion towards a particular deity or spiritual figure, such as Krishna, Rama, or Shiva. Through the practice of bhakti, Hindus seek to achieve union with the divine and experience a profound sense of oneness and interconnectedness with all beings. The practice of bhakti involves singing devotional songs, reciting mantras, performing puja or worship, and engaging in acts of selfless service or seva. Through the practice of bhakti, Hindus seek to experience a profound sense of oneness and interconnectedness with all beings and to cultivate a deep and abiding love towards the divine.

In Christianity, the concept of universal love is expressed through agape, which is often referred to as unconditional love. Agape entails extending love and compassion towards all individuals, regardless of their beliefs, actions, or backgrounds. It is believed to be the highest form of love in Christianity and is considered to be the kind of love that God has for humanity. Through the practice of agape, Christians aim to embody the teachings and love of Jesus, which include compassion, forgiveness, and understanding. Christians are encouraged to love their neighbors as they love themselves, to turn the other cheek when faced with adversity, and to pray for their enemies. In essence, the practice of agape seeks to promote greater compassion, forgiveness, and understanding in the world, and to embody the love and teachings of Jesus.

In Islam, the concept of universal love is known as Rahma, which means mercy. Muslims practice Rahma by extending compassion and kindness towards all beings, including oneself, loved ones, strangers, and even enemies. The practice of Rahma is believed to be one of the 99 names of God, and it is considered to be a fundamental aspect of Islam. The teachings of the Prophet Muhammad, which emphasize compassion, mercy, and justice, are embodied through the practice of Rahma. Muslims are encouraged to show mercy and kindness towards all beings, to give to charity, and to pray for guidance and forgiveness. Through the practice of Rahma, Muslims seek to promote greater peace, harmony, and understanding in the world.

While these spiritual traditions may have their own unique expressions of universal love, the essence of the practice remains the same. Universal love encourages individuals to extend compassion, kindness, and empathy towards all beings, regardless of their beliefs, actions, or backgrounds.

The practice of universal love can also serve as a powerful tool for personal transformation and growth. By cultivating a greater sense of empathy and compassion towards others, individuals can experience greater inner peace, happiness, and fulfillment. It can help people to embrace their own feelings and understand themselves on a deeper level.

Additionally, the practice of universal love can have a positive impact on society as a whole, promoting greater social harmony and understanding. By practicing universal love, individuals can overcome cultural and religious differences and promote greater acceptance, respect, and love between people of different backgrounds.

Moreover, the practice of universal love can be adapted to fit different cultural and religious contexts, making it a powerful tool for promoting greater understanding and connection between different communities. It can help people to embrace the beauty of diversity and promote the sense of unity that lies at the core of all spiritual traditions.

In conclusion, the practice of universal love is a fundamental aspect of many spiritual traditions. Whether through the practice of metta in Buddhism, bhakti in Hinduism, agape in Christianity, or rahma in Islam, the principle of universal love encourages individuals to extend compassion, kindness, and empathy towards all beings. By adapting this principle to fit different cultural and religious contexts, we can promote greater understanding, connection, and love in the world.

Chapter 5: Science of Universal Love

The practice of universal love is not only a fundamental aspect of many spiritual traditions but also has been the subject of scientific research in recent years. In this chapter, we will explore the scientific research on the benefits of practicing universal love, specifically through the practice of loving-kindness meditation.

Loving-kindness meditation is a practice that involves cultivating feelings of love, compassion, and kindness towards oneself and others. Through the practice of loving-kindness meditation, individuals can learn to extend these feelings towards all beings, including strangers and even difficult people. This practice has been shown to have numerous benefits for emotional and physical health.

Research has shown that the practice of loving-kindness meditation can reduce symptoms of depression, anxiety, and PTSD. A study published in the Journal of Clinical Psychology found that participants who practiced loving-kindness meditation for six weeks experienced significant reductions in symptoms of depression and anxiety compared to a control group. Additionally, a study published in the Journal of Traumatic Stress found that veterans with PTSD who practiced loving-kindness meditation experienced significant reductions in symptoms of PTSD and depression.

The practice of loving-kindness meditation can also have positive effects on physical health. A study published in the Journal of Alternative and Complementary Medicine found that participants who practiced loving-kindness meditation experienced significant reductions in inflammatory markers associated with chronic illnesses such as diabetes and heart disease.   Additionally, a study published in the Journal of Psychosomatic Research found that individuals who practiced loving-kindness meditation had improved cardiovascular function and decreased cortisol levels, a hormone associated with stress.

These studies suggest that the practice of universal love, specifically through the practice of loving-kindness meditation, can have a significant impact on emotional and physical health. By cultivating feelings of love, compassion, and kindness towards oneself and others, individuals can experience reduced symptoms of depression, anxiety, and PTSD, and improved physical health.

In conclusion, the scientific research on the benefits of practicing universal love, specifically through the practice of loving-kindness meditation, is promising. The practice of loving-kindness meditation can lead to improved emotional and physical health, such as reducing symptoms of depression, anxiety, and PTSD, and improving cardiovascular function and reducing inflammatory markers. By incorporating the practice of universal love into our daily lives, we can experience these benefits and promote greater wellbeing for ourselves and those around us.

Chapter 6: Overcoming Obstacles to Universal Love

While the practice of universal love has many benefits, it is not always easy to cultivate. There are common obstacles that can hinder the practice of universal love, such as fear, anger, and judgment. In this chapter, we will explore these obstacles and how to overcome them through mindfulness and other techniques.

Fear is a common obstacle to practicing universal love. Fear can prevent us from opening our hearts and extending love towards others. It is important to recognize and acknowledge our fears and the ways in which they prevent us from practicing universal love. Mindfulness techniques, such as breath awareness and body scans, can help us to identify and release our fears, allowing us to cultivate feelings of love and compassion.

Anger is another common obstacle to practicing universal love. When we are angry, it can be difficult to extend love and compassion towards others. It is important to recognize that anger is a normal human emotion and that it is possible to transform anger into love and compassion. Mindfulness techniques, such as loving-kindness meditation, can help us to transform our anger into love and compassion towards ourselves and others.

Judgment is also a common obstacle to practicing universal love. When we judge ourselves and others, we create barriers to love and compassion. It is important to recognize our judgments and to cultivate non-judgmental awareness. Mindfulness techniques, such as non-judgmental observation and self-compassion, can help us to overcome our judgments and to cultivate feelings of love and compassion.

Self-compassion is an important aspect of overcoming obstacles to practicing universal love. When we are kind and compassionate towards ourselves, we are better able to extend that kindness and compassion towards others. Self-compassion involves treating ourselves with kindness, recognizing our common humanity, and cultivating a sense of mindfulness towards our own experiences. By practicing self-compassion, we can overcome obstacles to universal love and cultivate greater wellbeing for ourselves and others.

In conclusion, while obstacles to practicing universal love exist, they can be overcome through mindfulness and other techniques. Fear, anger, and judgment can prevent us from practicing universal love, but through mindfulness and self-compassion, we can transform these obstacles into opportunities for greater love and

compassion. By cultivating universal love for ourselves and others,

we can experience greater wellbeing and promote greater

compassion and kindness in the world around us.

Chapter 7: Living a Life of Universal Love

Living a life of universal love is not a one-time decision or an overnight change. It requires ongoing effort, practice, and commitment. In this chapter, we will explore practical tips for integrating the practice of universal love into daily life and creating a more compassionate and connected society.

The first step towards living a life of universal love is to make it a habit. Just like any other habit, the more you practice it, the easier it becomes. Start by setting aside a few minutes each day to practice loving-kindness meditation or any other form of universal love that resonates with you. As you become more comfortable with the practice, try to incorporate it into your daily routine.

Another important aspect of living a life of universal love is to cultivate a sense of gratitude. Gratitude helps us focus on the positive aspects of our lives and helps us appreciate the people and things around us. Practice gratitude by keeping a gratitude journal, expressing gratitude to loved ones, or simply taking a moment to appreciate the beauty of nature.

Living a life of universal love also requires us to be mindful of our thoughts and actions. We should strive to be kind and compassionate to ourselves and others, even in difficult situations. When we encounter challenges, we should try to approach them with an open and non-judgmental attitude.

It is also essential to surround ourselves with like-minded individuals who share our values and beliefs. Joining a spiritual community or participating in group activities focused on universal love can be a great way to connect with others and deepen our practice.

Furthermore, living a life of universal love involves making a conscious effort to promote social justice and equality. We should work towards creating a society where all individuals are treated with respect and compassion, regardless of their race, gender, sexual orientation, or any other factor.

Living a life of universal love is not just about improving our own wellbeing but also creating a more peaceful and harmonious world for everyone. By cultivating universal love through daily practice, gratitude, mindfulness, and social action, we can create a more compassionate and connected society.

Chapter 8: The Power of Universal Love in Management

In today's fast-paced and competitive business world, many companies are realizing the importance of cultivating a positive and compassionate work environment. One of the most significant factors in creating such an environment is the practice of universal love, not only amongst employees but also amongst managers.

Great managers who practice universal love create a workplace culture that promotes respect, empathy, and collaboration. Employees who work under managers that practice universal love tend to feel valued and appreciated, leading to higher job satisfaction and employee loyalty. In contrast, employees who feel undervalued or unappreciated may be more likely to leave the company, leading to higher turnover rates and decreased productivity.

A great manager who practices universal love should lead by example, demonstrating kindness, compassion, and understanding towards their employees. This means showing interest in their lives outside of work, listening actively to their concerns, and providing support when needed. Managers who make an effort to connect with their employees on a personal level tend to build stronger relationships with them, leading to higher levels of trust and loyalty.

In addition, great managers who practice universal love should also be mindful of the work environment they create. They should foster an environment that promotes open communication, mutual respect, and trust. Such an environment allows employees to feel comfortable expressing their ideas and concerns without fear of retaliation, leading to increased creativity, innovation, and productivity.

Furthermore, managers who practice universal love should be proactive in promoting social justice and equality in the workplace. They should be aware of any biases they may have and take steps to address them. They should also strive to create a workplace that is inclusive and welcoming to individuals of all backgrounds, cultures, and identities.

In conclusion, the practice of universal love is not limited to personal relationships but can also be applied in the workplace. Great managers who practice universal love can create a work environment that promotes respect, empathy, and collaboration. Employees who work under such managers tend to feel valued and appreciated, leading to higher job satisfaction and employee loyalty. As such, the practice of universal love in management can lead to not only a more compassionate and connected workplace but also increased productivity and success for the company as a whole.

The practice of universal love in management can also lead to improved mental and emotional well-being for both managers and employees. When managers make an effort to create a positive and supportive work environment, they are likely to experience less stress and burnout. This, in turn, can lead to improved job satisfaction, better health outcomes, and increased productivity. Furthermore, when employees feel valued and appreciated by their managers, they are more likely to be motivated to perform at their best. They are also more likely to form positive relationships with their colleagues, leading to increased collaboration and teamwork. Such a work environment can also foster a sense of community and belonging, which can have positive effects on both personal and professional well-being.

It's important to note that the practice of universal love in management is not just about being nice or friendly to employees. It's about creating a culture that values empathy, respect, and compassion. This means that managers must be willing to have difficult conversations and make tough decisions when necessary.

However, by doing so with kindness and understanding, they can maintain a positive work environment that encourages growth and development.

Moreover, practicing universal love in management can also have a positive impact on the company's bottom line. Studies have shown that companies with high levels of employee engagement and satisfaction tend to be more profitable and successful. When employees feel valued and appreciated, they are more likely to be loyal to the company and less likely to leave, reducing turnover and associated costs.

The practice of universal love in management can lead to numerous benefits, including improved mental and emotional well-being for managers and employees, increased productivity and success for the company, and a more positive and supportive work environment. Great managers who practice universal love create a workplace culture that promotes respect, empathy, and collaboration, leading to higher job satisfaction and employee loyalty. By integrating the practice of universal love into management, companies can create a more compassionate and connected workplace, leading to increased success and growth for all.

Research has shown that there are several business outcomes associated with having managers who practice universal love in their management style. Firstly, employees who feel valued and supported by their managers are more likely to be engaged and productive at work. According to a study by Gallup, companies with highly engaged workforces outperform their peers by 147% in earnings per share. When managers practice universal love, they create a positive work environment that promotes employee engagement and satisfaction.

Secondly, having managers who practice universal love can reduce employee turnover and associated costs. According to a study by the Society for Human Resource Management, it can cost up to 50-60% of an employee's salary to replace them. When managers create a positive and supportive work environment, employees are more likely to stay with the company for the long term, reducing turnover and associated costs.

Thirdly, companies with high levels of employee engagement and satisfaction tend to have better financial performance. According to a study by the Harvard Business Review, companies with engaged employees outperform those without by 202%. This can be attributed to factors such as increased productivity, innovation, and customer satisfaction.

Fourthly, having managers who practice universal love can improve customer satisfaction and loyalty. When employees are engaged and motivated, they are more likely to provide high-quality customer service and build positive relationships with customers. This, in turn, can lead to increased customer satisfaction and loyalty.

Finally, having managers who practice universal love can improve the company's reputation and brand image. When a company is known for having a positive and supportive work environment, it can attract top talent and customers who value ethical and compassionate business practices.

In conclusion, there are several business outcomes associated with having managers who practice universal love, including increased employee engagement and productivity, reduced turnover and associated costs, better financial performance, improved customer satisfaction and loyalty, and a positive reputation and brand image. Companies that prioritize a culture of compassion and empathy in their management style can benefit in numerous ways, both for their employees and for their bottom line.